X Means Ten
On the Face of Big Ben

A London Alphabet

Written & Illustrated by Hazel Spire

For all my London cousins

Illustrations are painted by Hazel Spire

Photos within book are taken by Hazel Spire

Author photo by Dana Davis

Porthole ("Y" page), magnifying glass ("A Closer Look" page), title page picture of Big Ben, and front cover picture of Big Ben are from Pixabay (royalty free stock photos)

Editing and interior design by Britta Ann Meadows (Peas in a Pod Editing & Design)

Published by Raemark Press

346 Road 21, Sedan, Kansas, 67361

www.hazelspire.com

Library of Congress Control Number: 2018954111

ISBN: 978-1-7325090-1-6

X Means Ten on the Face of Big Ben

This is the tale of a famous city;

Some parts ugly, some parts pretty.

From A to Z, from new to old,

The wonders of London will now unfold.

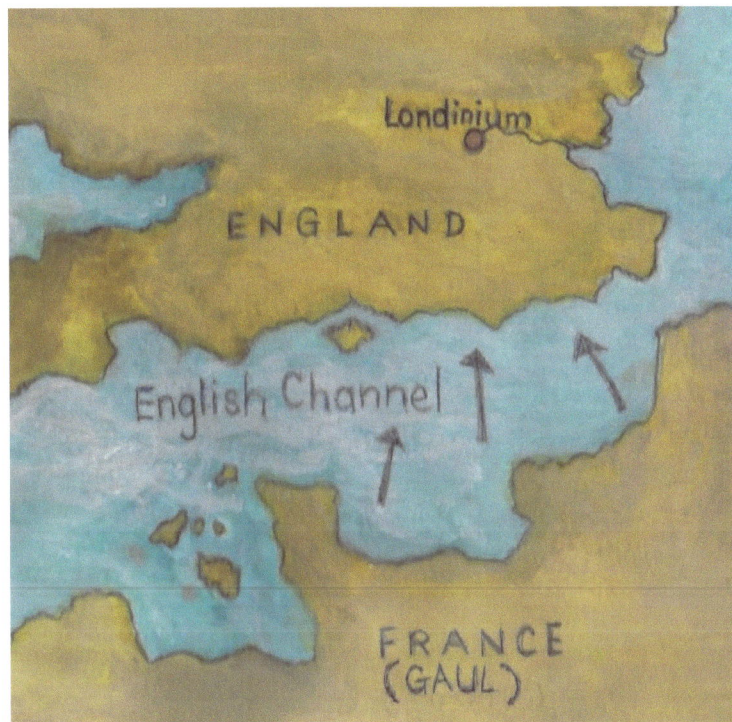

The Roman invasion of 43 A.D.

A is for A.D. FORTY-THREE,

The year the Romans crossed the sea.

They beat the British tribes and showed

The way to build a good, straight road.

Europe's ARTISTS came to stay—
Van Gogh, Pissarro, and Monet.

Camille Pissarro

Anne Boleyn

ANNE was Henry's second wife;
At Tower Green she lost her life.

B is for BOBBY...

19th century police helmet

BEATLES, too...

Paul, John, George, & Ringo

21ˢᵗ century double-decker

BUS, the BATTLE of Waterloo…

Boots designed by the Duke of Wellington

And a BRIDGE that sank in clay;
Its bricks were flown to the USA.

London Bridge, upriver toward Southwark

C is a CLIPPER, the CUTTY SARK,

The Cutty Sark

Speechmaker in Hyde Park

And Speakers' CORNER in Hyde Park.

Also, CROWNS for a queen or king;
History lives beneath the bling!

Imperial State Crown

D is for DOCK, where you will find DRAKE'S galleon, the *Golden Hind*.

Golden Hind *at St. Mary Overie dock*

And D is DIANA, a young princess.

Who are her two sons? Can you guess?

Diana, Princess of Wales

E is for EGBERT, ancient ruler,

Egbert, first King of the English

But in our time, nothing is cooler

Than riding the EYE— looking down,

To east, to west, all over town!

The London Eye

F is FOOD: toad-in-the-hole,

Trifle, scones, and Dover sole.

FISH in markets, fresh from ships;

Eat it battered, with peas and chips.

"Fish and chips"

Guido (Guy) Fawkes, 1605

Fireworks pop on the Fifth of November!

That's when Londoners remember

Guy FAWKES' plot to kill King James;

Guy's effigy goes up in flames.

G is the GLOBE, where Shakespeare plays

Are staged, as in Renaissance days,

Built as before, of plaster and wood;

Down in front, the GROUNDLINGS stood.

Shakespeare's Globe Theatre

And G is a GREAT PLAGUE, deathly dire,

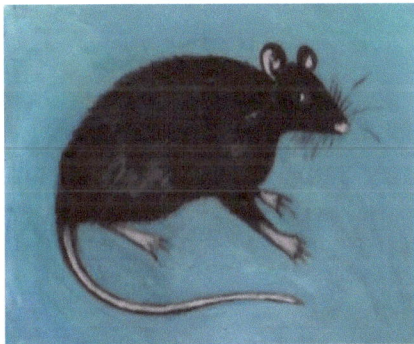

Black rat that spread the Plague

The Great Fire of London, 1666

Banished by the famed GREAT FIRE!

H is for HOUSES OF PARLIAMENT,

Houses of Parliament in the style of Monet

And HORSE GUARDS, royal regiment.

Royal Horse Guards helmet

I is for ISAMBARD BRUNEL

Designing railways, ships as well.

Isambard Kingdom Brunel

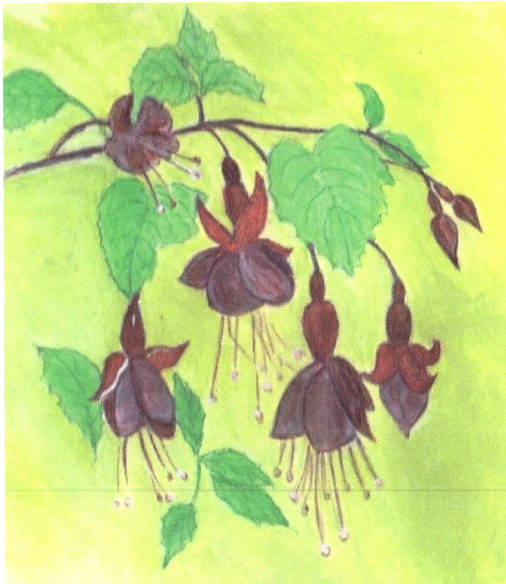

Fuchsias (ballerinas) grow in flowerbeds

Flowers once filled ISLINGTON,

Lambeth fields, and Paddington.

J is for the JUBILEE—

The Queen's Diamond Jubilee celebrated 60 years of her reign.

Party time, with cakes and tea!

JOHN NASH built homes in stately rows.

Marble Arch, designed by John Nash

JESTERS joked in palace shows.

A court jester, or joker

K is for KINGS who've come and gone—

Charles, William, George, and John.

Charles II

Silent K is a cabbie's test,

Called the KNOWLEDGE, to be the best.

A black cab, or Hackney carriage

L is for LIONS that face four ways,

While Nelson dreams of glory days.

One of four bronze lions created by Edwin Landseer,
located in Trafalgar Square

And L is LEFT, the side Brits drive;

Remember this to arrive alive!

"Keep Left" traffic sign

M is for MADAME TUSSAUDS MUSEUM

Of waxworks. Millions flock to see 'em—

Heroes and villains, present and past.

See one move? Find an exit, fast!

Anna Maria (Marie) Tussaud

Florence Nightingale

N was a NURSE, Miss NIGHTINGALE.

At thirty-four, the first female

To supervise a nursing team;

Improving hospitals was her dream.

O is the OVAL cricket ground;

Wood on leather, summer sound...

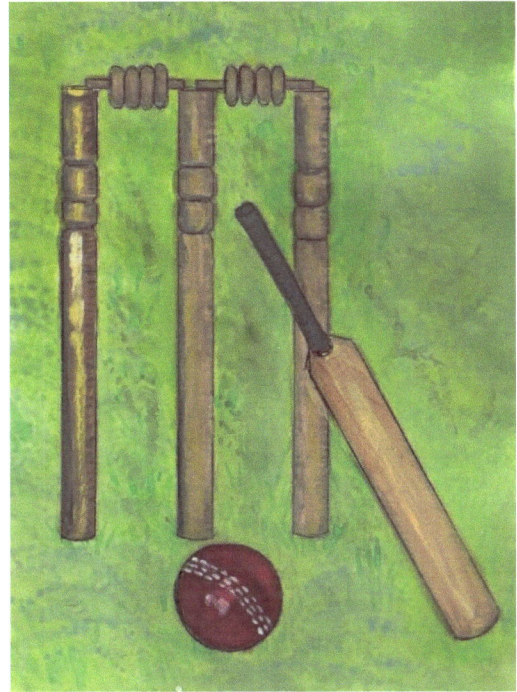

Cricket ball, bat, and stumps (wicket)

Cleopatra's Needle on the Embankment

And an Egyptian OBELISK.

Transporting it was quite a risk.

On OXFORD STREET, buy a souvenir;

Buses and taxis rush through here.

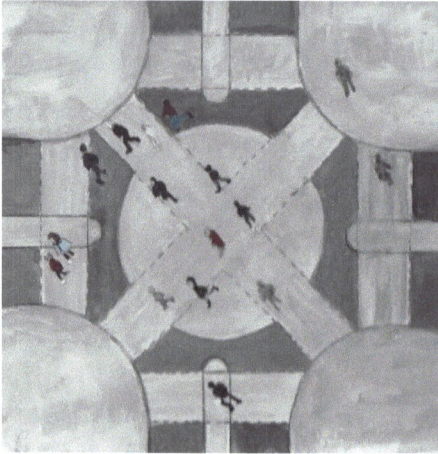

Diagonal pedestrian crossing

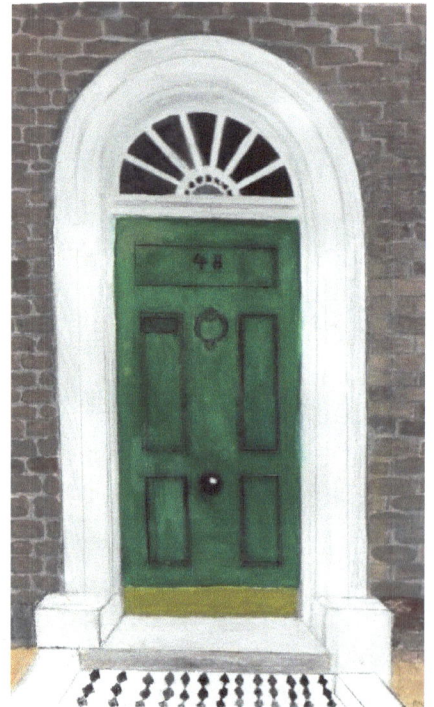

Charles Dickens Museum, Doughty St.

See Charles Dickens' house? On the list

Of books he wrote is *OLIVER TWIST*.

P is for PIGEONS, pecking bread,

Funny, messy, and overfed

By crowds at PICCADILLY, where

Anteros' arrows pierce the air.

A pigeon may be a pest—or a hero!

Poet/playwright William Shakespeare

P is also POUNDS and PENCE;

Currency, like dollars and cents.

Meet POETS and POLITICIANS grand,

At a PORTRAIT GALLERY near the Strand.

Q is for QUILL, a feather pen

For educated women and men...

Quill and ink, important for 1500 years

Also QUOITS, a game with rings...

Set of quoits with rope rings

Queen Elizabeth I,
Ann Boleyn's daughter

And QUEENS; some were married to kings.

R is for RALEIGH, boldly dressed,

Who found tobacco, way out West...

One of six ravens at the Tower of London

Sir Walter Raleigh

Also RAVENS, sleek and black.

If they leave, will they ever come back?

S is ST. PAUL'S with curving dome,

St. Paul's Cathedral on Ludgate Hill

And SOUTHWARK, writer Chaucer's home,
On the SOUTH BANK; here people meet
For shows, events, a bite to eat.

City Hall, new building on the South Bank

T is the THAMES, which flows for miles;

TOTTENHAM COURT ROAD, near St. Giles...

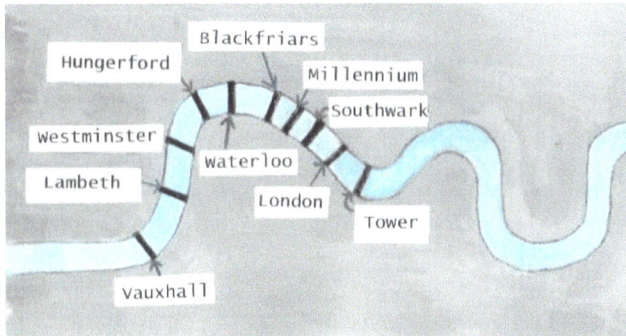

Ten of the bridges that cross the Thames

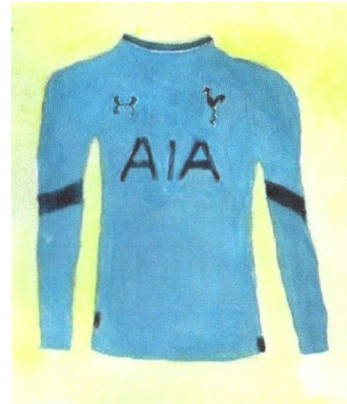

Tottenham Hotspur
goalkeeper shirt

Also the TUBE, a transit system:

All those stations! Who can list 'em?

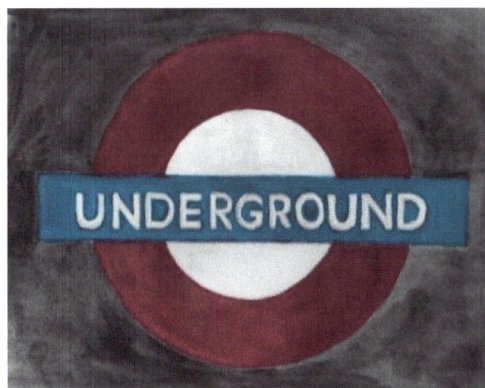

Sign at entrance to a Tube train station

National flag of the United Kingdom

U is for the UNION JACK…

And UMBRELLA. Use it, or wear a mac!

Jonas Hanway with his invention

V is for VENDORS, touting wares:

Watches, matches, cherries, pears.

18ᵗʰ century cherry seller

Bust of Queen Victoria

VICTORIA reigned for sixty-four years,

An age of steam and engineers.

W is when two WORLD WARS

Kept enemies from England's shores.

Shortest bird for the smallest coin

British fighter aircraft, the Spitfire

The bird on farthing coins is a WREN.

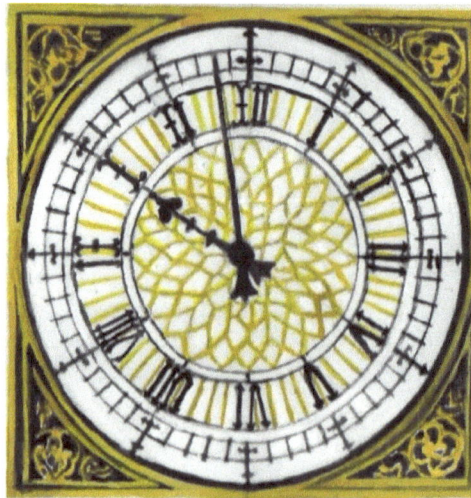

One of the clock tower's four faces

X means TEN on the face of Big Ben...

And X is XYLEM, deep in trees.

Escape to a park, enjoy the breeze.

Horse chestnuts for a game of conkers!

Y is a YEOMAN WARDER guide,

Who wears his uniform with pride.

Yeoman warder, or Beefeater

And Y can be YOU, if you travel there;

Take the QM2, or go by air.

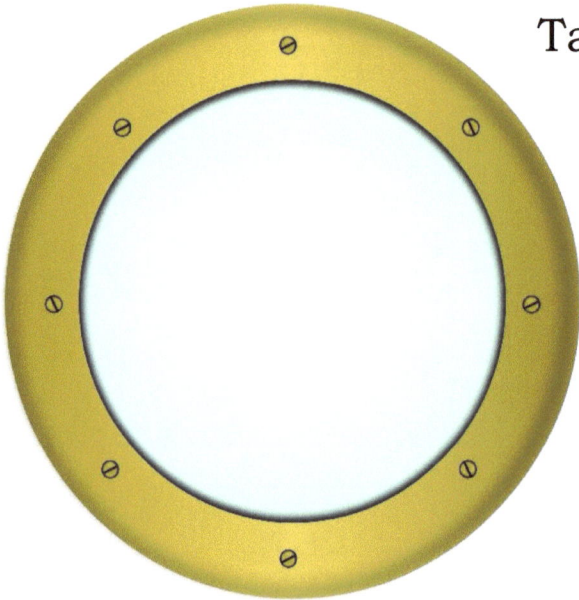

Attach a picture of yourself traveling on the QM2!

Z is for ZEBRAS at London ZOO,

With monkeys, giraffes, and a kinkajou.

No two zebras have the same markings

WWII Kindertransport children at Liverpool Street Station

Tower Bridge

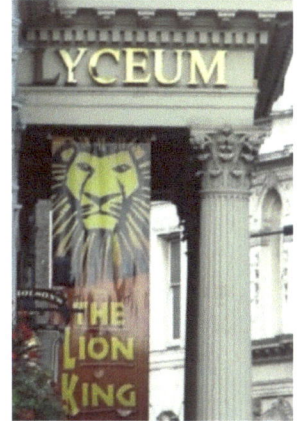

Lion King at the Lyceum Theatre

From A to ZED, or A to ZEE,

London offers lots to see...

And most of it is free!

Sphinx, with London Eye

Kensington Palace

Passenger boat named for Sir Charles Blyth

A CLOSER LOOK

London, in South East England, is the capital of the United Kingdom (Britain) and the largest city in Europe. Eight million people from diverse cultures live there, and 30 million tourists visit each year. London hosted the Summer Olympic Games for the third time in 2012.

A

A.D. stands for the Latin *Anno Domini* (*in the year of our Lord*, or after the birth of Christ). Emperor Claudius sent an army to invade Britain. The southern part became a Roman province, with *Londinium* as its capital. Roads were built on a foundation of clay, chalk, and gravel with flat stones sloped toward the edges for runoff.

Artists Claude Monet and Camille Pissarro fled to London in 1870, when the Franco-Prussian War began. Monet painted reflections on the River Thames, while Pissarro created neighborhood scenes. In 1873, Vincent Van Gogh left Holland to work for his uncle in London. From letters we learn details of his life in London—such as the purchase of a top hat.

In 1533, **Anne Boleyn** married King Henry VIII. In 1536, she was beheaded by the State. Her daughter Elizabeth became Queen in 1558. Tower Green is a space within the Tower of London where several historical figures died, including two of Henry's other wives.

B

London policemen are named **bobbies** for Sir Robert Peel, who set up a Metropolitan Police Force in 1829. The uniform was dark blue with a stovepipe hat, replaced in 1863 by a Prussian-style helmet, minus the spike.

The **Beatles** began their musical career in Liverpool, but made most of their recordings in London. Fans take walking tours to see their homes, studios, and movie settings. The British Library contains handwritten lyrics to ten of their songs.

By 1911, the horse-drawn omnibus had made way for the motor **bus**. The London General Operating Company painted theirs red, the color for which double-deck city buses are known today. In 2012, a bus with hybrid technology was introduced.

Britain and her Allies defeated Napoleon Bonaparte at the **Battle of Waterloo** (near Brussels) in 1815. Victory was marked by a bridge, a train terminus, and a statue of the Duke of Wellington.

"London Bridge is Falling Down" is a nursery rhyme that probably refers to the stone bridge begun in Henry II's reign. For 500 years it was the only bridge across the River Thames, but needed constant repairs. When the bridge that replaced it sank, an American businessman bought it to rebuild in Arizona. The present-day London Bridge opened in 1973. Do not confuse it with Tower Bridge, farther downriver.

C

In the 19th century, wind-powered **clipper** ships carried tea from China and wool from Australia, along with other goods, to England. The only one left today, the ***Cutty Sark***, was among the fastest, reaching 17 knots. After a long career, she was refurbished and reopened at Greenwich in 2012.

Speaker's Corner is near Marble Arch, at the north east tip of 350-acre Hyde Park. Here people have been free to express views on any subject for 200 years. They used to stand on a crate or ladder to be seen and heard, but in 2017 this was outlawed for safety reasons. Every Sunday, crowds gather to listen and heckle, or argue. Famous past orators include Karl Marx and George Orwell.

Items used in coronation ceremonies since Charles II make up the **Crown Jewels**. They are on display at the Tower of London, having survived fire and attempts at theft. No gem carries so much legend as the Koh-i-Noor Diamond, mined in India long before Christ. It was passed down through many dynasties until it reached Queen Victoria's hands in 1850.

D

Francis Drake was the first Englishman to sail around the world. After the three-year voyage, he was knighted by Queen Elizabeth I on board his flagship, the *Golden Hind.* A replica launched in 1973 lies at **St. Mary Overies Dock**. It sailed with 1,000 vessels in the Jubilee Pageant of 2012.

Lady Diana Spencer married Prince Charles, heir to the throne, in 1981. They divorced in 1996. She died in 1997 after a car crash in Paris. Admirers remember Diana's fashions and her charity work with children. To spell the names of her sons, unscramble these letters: IALMWLI and ARHYR.

E

Egbert ruled the West Saxons from 829 to 839. He then became sovereign of Kent, Sussex, Surrey, and Essex in southwestern England. Egbert's grandson was King Alfred the Great.

The **London Eye** is like a giant bicycle wheel, 394 feet across, on the south bank of the Thames. It opened to the public in 2000. The wheel's movement (0.6 mph) symbolized the turn of the century and millennium. 800 people can ride in its 32 capsules, with views for 25 miles on a clear day, even as far as Windsor Castle.

F

Food: "Toad-in-the-hole" refers to pork chops or sausages baked in Yorkshire pudding. Trifle is a dessert of sponge set in fruity gelatin, topped with custard and cream. Traditional scones are round, light, and served with Devonshire cream and strawberries. Dover sole is one of many saltwater **fish** caught around Britain. Billingsgate Market has sold fish since the 16th century. For 150 years, a popular takeout meal has been fish and chips: battered fillets of plaice, cod, or haddock, with fried potatoes, all sprinkled with salt and malt vinegar.

In 1605, conspirators led by **Guy Fawkes** moved 2-3 dozen barrels of gunpowder into a cellar under the House of Lords, intending to blow up James I's government. Eight men were caught and executed for treason. On Bonfire Night (November 5), children burn Fawkes's likeness made of stuffed clothes, vowing never to forget the Plot.

G

The Renaissance was a renewed passion for the arts in Elizabeth I's reign. William Shakespeare's comedies, tragedies, and histories were presented at the **Globe Theatre**, built in 1598. Poor people (**groundlings**) paid a penny to stand near the stage; the rich sat in galleries. In 1613, the Globe burned down when the roof caught fire. It was rebuilt and used until 1642. In the 20th century, American actor Sam Wanamaker dreamed of recreating the playhouse, and it opened in 1997. This one has fire exits and sprinklers!

The **Great Plague** (Bubonic Plague) broke out repeatedly across Europe in the middle Ages. The song "Ring a Ring o' Roses" refers to symptoms, deterrents, and results of this disease. Whole families died, and were taken on carts for burial in pits. London's last big epidemic was in 1665.

The **Great Fire** started in Pudding Lane in 1666 and spread to half the city. It took three days to put out, but killed most of the rats whose fleas carried the Plague. After this, all buildings had to be built of stone or brick.

H

The **Houses of Parliament** were built for William Rufus as England's seat of government. A fire in 1834 destroyed all but Westminster Hall. The present-day buildings, designed by Sir Charles Barry, were erected in 1840-70. Their best-known feature is the clock tower, renamed the Elizabeth Tower.

The Queen's **Household Cavalry** is on daily duty at **Horse Guards Arch**, the entrance to Buckingham Palace. It is made up of two regiments—the Life Guards, and the Blues and Royals. Ceremonies have barely changed in 500 years. The Household Cavalry serves in wars, as well as peacekeeping and humanitarian operations.

I

Isambard Kingdom Brunel worked with his father on the Thames Tunnel—the first tunnel under a river. He designed 25 railway lines, more than 100 bridges, and three steam ships. The *SS Great Britain* was the first iron-hulled passenger liner with a screw propeller. Isambard Brunel rebuilt Paddington Station for the 1851 Great Exhibition. He also sent a pre-fab field army hospital to the Crimean War. Thousands of railway workers attended his funeral in 1859.

London is divided into boroughs. Before 1800, many of these were woodlands or quiet villages like **Islington**, far from the center. Gradually the city expanded. Factories and houses sprang up along roads previously used for taking sheep to the meat market, and donkeys or handcarts laden with produce. Highways, rail, canals, and buses enabled people and goods to move more easily. Outdoor stalls today sell a range of plants. One of the most popular is the Columbia Road flower market.

J

A **Jubilee** marks an important anniversary in the monarch's reign. 25 years is Silver, 50 is Golden, and 60 is Diamond—which Queen Elizabeth II reached in June 2012. Street parties were held around Britain, with music, food, and bunting. The official emblem for the Jubilee was drawn by a ten-year-old girl, winner of a contest.

The graceful designs of 19th century architect **John Nash** can be seen in such London streets as Trafalgar Square and Cumberland Terrace. He also helped to enlarge Buckingham Palace. Nash's style is called Neo-Classical. He worked with landscape artists, so that homes would blend with their surroundings.

Dressed in a colorful costume and hat with bells, the **jester** provided entertainment for a ruler or nobleman. An ordinary cowherd might be invited to sit at the royal table, if he could sing, dance, or juggle. A jester was allowed to insult the king, when done with humor and wit. In Europe, this custom lasted until the late 18th century.

K

Since 1066, England has had two **kings** named Charles, two named James, four Williams, six Georges, eight Henrys, eight Edwards, three Richards, and one John. George III was in power during the Revolutionary War with America. George VI was the father of the present Queen. Next in line is her firstborn son, Prince Charles, followed by his son William and grandson George.

To earn a badge in London, taxi drivers have to pass the **Knowledge**—a series of difficult interviews and tests. They must name the shortest route from one point to another (including one-way systems) and know tourist sites, shows, and events. No satellite navigation device is allowed! The fastest and cheapest form of transport in 17th/18th-century London was the sedan chair, a seat on two poles carried by two chairmen.

L

Nelson's column was built in 1843 to commemorate victory over Napoleon's fleets in 1805. A statue of Admiral Horatio Nelson, three times larger than life, stands atop a granite column in Trafalgar Square. At its base are four bronze **lions**, each 20 feet by 22 feet, cast from captured French guns. Nelson joined the navy at age 12 and became a captain at 20. He lost an arm, the sight in one eye, and, ultimately, his life, in sea battles. The height of the column is 170 feet. It was steam-cleaned in 2006.

A mounted Roman soldier held the reins in his left hand and rode on the **left** side of the highway. This kept his right arm free to reach for his sword if needed against an oncoming stranger. Medieval knights did the same, and the custom continued for horse-drawn buggies and the automobile. Former British colonies still drive on the left.

M

Madame Tussaud made wax sculptures in 18th century Paris. Her first solo exhibition was in London, near today's **museum**. Take a selfie with Lady Gaga, Olympic athletes, Einstein, movie stars, presidents—

even superheroes, Shrek, and Star Wars characters! A figure might take 800 hours to create. After 150 measurements are made, clay is added to a metal armature. A plaster mold is formed in sections. Liquid wax (for head) or fiberglass (body) is poured into the mold. Artists paint the skin and acrylic eyes and teeth. Hairs are poked into the wax and styled, taking five weeks per head.

N

Florence Nightingale (1820-1910) was called "the lady with the lamp" when she worked 20 hours a day at a British army hospital during the Crimean War. Her parents didn't think nursing a suitable job for ladies, but Florence felt called by God. Her team of 38 **nurses** cared for sick and wounded soldiers. They provided food, bandages, beds, clean water, blankets—and Jimmy, a pet tortoise! Thanks to Florence's 13,000 letters, plus 200 books and papers, money poured in to improve hospitals in many countries. See Jimmy's shell and more at the Florence Nightingale Museum.

O

The **Kennington Oval** used to be a cabbage patch bordered by an oval road. In 1845, it was transformed into the home of Surrey Cricket Club. Cricket is played by two 11-player teams who take turns (innings) to bat or to bowl. Players wear white shirts, trousers, and sweaters. After a defeat by Australia in 1882, an obituary for English cricket appeared in the *Sporting Times*! Since then, the two teams have competed for an urn representing the ashes of English cricket. Plans are underway to redevelop the Oval to hold a crowd of 40,000.

Cleopatra's Needle is an **obelisk**—a tall prism with a pyramid on top—standing 68 feet tall on the Embankment. It was made of granite in ancient Egypt; on each side is a bronze Sphinx. The British acquired the obelisk after their final victory over Napoleon. Funds were raised to ship the 180-ton obelisk to London via the Bay of Biscay, where it almost sank. At the base of the Needle are the names of six men who drowned in the rescue.

Mingling with the crowds on **Oxford Street**, who would guess that this was once the route from Newgate Prison to the gallows at Tyburn? It is now the busiest street in Europe, with a mile-and-a-half of shops, including Selfridge's department store. Oxford Street is in the West End of London. Each November, a celebrity turns on the Christmas lights. In 2009 a diagonal pedestrian crossing, inspired by one in Tokyo, was placed where Oxford Street meets Regent Street.

Like his fictional characters **Oliver Twist** and Pip, Charles Dickens (1812-1870) knew from a young age how it felt to be poor. His writing skills gave him a chance to improve his life, while condemning injustice and cruelty. One of Dickens' London homes—48 Doughty Place, where his two daughters were born—is now a museum. Charles Dickens is buried in Westminster Abbey.

P

To reduce the number of feral **pigeons**, fines and signs around London keep people from feeding them. The birds still find leftovers in lunch wrappers in public places. Pigeons carry diseases and damage monuments with their feces. But they can be heroes, too. 32 PDSA Dickin medals for gallantry were awarded to Royal Air Force messenger pigeons that saved lives during World War II!

Piccadilly Circus in central London is not what we imagine a circus to be. It was named for a traffic roundabout and for *piccadils*, frilly collars made by a 17th century tailor who lived in the area. Friends gather on the steps beneath a fountain and a winged figure of Anteros. This statue represented the Angel of Christian charity when built in 1893, to honor Lord Shaftesbury's work with the poor. The area is lit up at night with flashing neon advertisements.

UK money went decimal in 1971. One **pound** is made up of 100 **pence**. There are 1p, 2p, 5p, 10p, 20p, 50p, £1, and £2 coins. The paper *pound note* was phased out in the 1980s. Before 1971, a pound equaled 240 pence or 20 shillings. Other coins were the farthing, halfpenny, three-penny bit, sixpence, florin, and half-crown. All coins and bills minted after 1953 bear the image of Queen Elizabeth II. In 1999, Britain voted to keep its currency, instead of adopting the Euro.

Britain's National Portrait Gallery is near Trafalgar Square. It was built in 1856 to house paintings and sculptures of the nation's important people. The walls are filled with faces and figures—from Anne Boleyn to Shakespeare to Dame Maggie Smith, whose movie roles include a professor in the *Harry Potter* series. As with most London galleries, admission is free. Around the corner is a busy street called Strand; 800 years ago it was a sandy path along the Thames.

Q

Our word *pen* is from *penna*, Latin for *feather*. Roman reed pens were replaced by pens made from **quills**, flight feathers of birds, usually from a goose or crow. The tip was hardened in hot sand and shaped with a knife. England raised geese for the purpose, but one quill lasted only a week. Thousands of quills had to be imported from Russia and elsewhere. They were needed for maps, ships' logs, letters, novels, Biblical manuscripts, illustrations, and legal documents.

Similar to horseshoes, or hoopla at the fairground, **quoits** has been played for more than 1,000 years. Rings of iron (or rope or rubber) are tossed over target spikes stuck in soft clay. King Edward III, worried that men would lose their skills in archery, outlawed quoits. But by the 15th century it was legal and popular again. Official rules were developed in the 1900s, with regional variations.

Historically, the way to become a **queen** in England was to marry a king—for the title of queen consort, though not the power—or to inherit the throne when no close male relative was available. A man who marries a queen does not become a king, but a prince consort. Queen Elizabeth I never married. Queen Victoria's husband was Prince Albert. The present-day queen is married to Prince Philip, the Duke of Edinburgh. In 2013 the law changed, allowing a monarch's first child, whether boy or girl, to be next in line for the throne.

R

Explorer, poet, and soldier **Sir Walter Raleigh** sent ships to the land he had named Virginia. They returned with potato and tobacco. Raleigh introduced these plants to England and Ireland, but his quest for gold failed. He fell in and out of favor with Elizabeth I, and later James I. Knighted in 1585, he was imprisoned in the Tower of London twice, and executed for treason in 1618. His courtly manners live on in the relay game Sir Walter Raleigh, played in pairs. The boy lays down newspaper for the girl to step on, gradually moving it toward the finish line.

A **raven** is a large bird in the crow family. Six (plus 1 spare) live at the Tower of London, which has stood for 900 years. According to legend, if the ravens leave, the Tower will fall, and disaster will follow! The birds are cared for by the Ravenmaster. One wing is painlessly clipped to unbalance flight; a few have escaped in the past. All but one fled, scared by the bombs, during World War II. The ravens have traditional names like Thor and Merlin. They eat raw meat, biscuits, scraps, and a weekly egg; sheep hearts are a special treat!

S

A cathedral dedicated to **Saint Paul** stands at the highest point in London. Designed by Sir Christopher Wren in the 17ᵗʰ century, it replaced earlier buildings lost to fire and decay. 560 steps take you through the Whispering Gallery to the top of the Dome, 366 feet high. Nelson's funeral and Prince Charles' wedding were held at St. Paul's. Thousands of Londoners attended services here to thank God at the end of World War II. The cathedral is also an outreach center to meet people's needs in the parish.

For centuries, the borough of **Southwark** (SUTH-erk) was known for its churches, hospitals, bridges, inns, and theatres. From here, 14ᵗʰ-century pilgrims set out on a four-day journey that Chaucer wrote about in *The Canterbury Tales*. The **South Bank** of the Thames is now a popular district containing the Royal Festival Hall, Shakespeare's Globe, the Hayward and Tate Modern galleries, and restaurants.

T

The **Thames** River begins in the Cotswold Hills and ends in the North Sea, 200 miles to the east. It has always been important to London, and has been described as "liquid history." In the 18ᵗʰ century, London was the world's busiest port. By 1864, the summer of the Great Stink, pollution had killed all the fish and spread cholera among residents. Engineers built a sewer system and raised the banks to create a deep channel for faster flow. Today, clean water makes the Thames popular for sightseeing, commuting, and recreation.

The 150-year-old rail system beneath the streets of London is called the **Tube**, or the Underground. It boasts 270-plus stops, 400 miles of track, and 400 escalators carrying one billion passengers a year! People slept there during the Blitz in World War II; 2,400 gallons of tea and cocoa were served nightly, along with food and entertainment. The newest section, the Elizabeth line, is a high-speed service linking east and west.

One of the Tube's busiest stations is **Tottenham Court Road**, on the Central Line. The street above it was a highway mentioned in the Domesday Book. Its shops sell home furnishings and electronics. The local football (soccer) team is **Tottenham Hotspur** (nicknamed Spurs), with a new stadium built in 2018. St. Giles-in-the-Fields church, known for its hospitality, has stood in the West End for 900 years.

U

The Union Flag—or **Union Jack** when flown from a ship—is the national flag of the United Kingdom. It contains three previous flags—a red cross on white for England (St. George), a white X (*saltire*) on blue for Scotland (St. Andrew), and a red X on white for Ireland (St. Patrick). The Welsh dragon is not included, as Wales was not a kingdom when it joined England.

Sunshades protected royal heads in ancient Egypt and Persia. Ladies carried parasols in 18th century Europe. But Jonas Hanway was the first man to carry an **umbrella** against the rain. People laughed at him—until the idea caught on! Manufacturers replaced the whalebone ribs with steel, and the oilcloth canopy with nylon. A raincoat is often called a "mac" after Charles Mackintosh, a Scottish chemist who found a way to waterproof clothes with liquefied rubber in 1823. Almost two feet of rain falls on London each year.

V

If you could go back 300-500 years, you would hear the loud, musical cries of many **vendors**: "Any knives to grind? Chairs to mend? Buy a new love song! Mackerel, four for a shilling! Ripe cherries! Sweet strawberries! Primroses, tuppence a bunch!" Similar cries echo in the street markets of London today, although some have moved indoors.

18-year-old Princess **Victoria** became Queen in 1837. She died in 1901. Her reign brought antiseptics, anesthetics, X-rays, electric lighting, and steam trains. London was overcrowded as people moved in from the country. The 1870 Education Act offered free school, but many children still worked in factories.

W

On the second Sunday in November, Britain honors those killed or wounded in **World Wars** I (1914–18) and II (1939–45). The Queen lays the first wreath at the Cenotaph in Whitehall. Paper poppies are worn to represent flowers that grew on battlegrounds; the leaf points to 11:00, when World War I ended (November 11, 1918).

The farthing, one-fourth of a penny, was part of English money for over 600 years. A tiny bird called a **wren** appeared on the farthing in 1937 and stayed until the much-loved coin was withdrawn in 1960.

X

Could you say you have seen Big Ben? Yes and no. It started out as a nickname for the largest bell in the clock tower, but came to mean the tower itself. Each of the four faces is 23 feet across. Its ornate numerals are Roman: I, II, III, IV, V, VI, VII, IX, **X**, XI, and XII. Each one is 2 feet high. The hands are 9 feet and 14 feet. In August 2017, the bell was silenced for four years (apart from special occasions), so repairs could be done without deafening the workers.

Xylem strengthens a plant and carries water and minerals up through the stem system. Ancient oaks, chestnuts, beeches, English roses, etc., abound in London's eight royal parks and many smaller parks. Plenty of green space—"London's lung"—is available for sunbathing, boating, walking, skateboarding, and picnics.

Y

Twelve **Yeoman Warders** are on daily duty at the Tower of London, guiding visitors to items of interest. They have held the same gate-locking ceremony every night for 700 years! The red-and-gold costume worn on special occasions dates back to Tudor times, when the Tower was a prison. But the more comfortable, everyday uniform of dark blue and red is from the Victorian era. Yeoman Warders are also known as Beefeaters.

If **you** fly from a US city to one of London's airports, the journey takes eight hours or more. Travelers with time and money might go on the *Queen Mary 2*, a luxury cruise ship with 14 decks and 10 restaurants, sailing from New York to Southampton in seven days. London can be reached by rail or road, but a congestion charge is in effect for cars during business hours.

Z

Regent's Park **Zoo**, which opened in the 1800s, is the oldest scientific zoo in the world. Each of its 19,000 inhabitants is weighed annually! The kinkajou, named Forrest, is a relative of the raccoon.

For Americans, the last letter of the alphabet is pronounced *zee*, while British people call it *zed*.

BIBLIOGRAPHY

Best, Nicholas   *The Kings and Queens of England*

Betjeman, John, *et al*   Weidenfield & Nicholson, London 1995

                                        Flower of Cities: A Book of London

                                        (Studies & sketches by 22 authors)

                                        Max Parrish, London 1949

Felix, Paul & Charlton, Bill   *A Year on the Thames*

                                        Alan Sutton, UK and US 1990

Ferrier, Neil   *The Queen Elizabeth Coronation Souvenir*

                                        L.T.A. Robinson Ltd. London 1953

Hume, Ruth (Fox)   *Florence Nightingale*

                                        Random House, 1960

Morris, Neil   *Great Cities through the Ages: London*

                                        Enchanted Lion Press/McRae Books, NY 2004

Slade, Fitzgerald   *Cries of London: Arranged for piano and voice*

                                        Engravings by F. Wheatly, 1795

                                        Associated Newspapers Ltd, London 1955

Thurley, Simon, et al   *Tower of London: The Official Guidebook, 1996*

INTERNET

www.aviewoncities.com/london.htm   www.riverthames.co.uk

www.elizabethan-era.org.uk   www.royalparks.org.uk

www.florence-nightingale.co.uk   www.shakespearesglobe.com

www.historic-uk.com   www.stpauls.co.uk

www.hrp.org.uk (Historic Royal Palaces)   www.npg.org.uk (National Portrait Gallery)

ltmuseum.co.uk (London Transport)   www.victorianweb.org

www.projectbritain.com   www.zsl.org (Zoological Society of London

Also by Hazel Spire

Catching the Trade Winds: Poetry of Time and Tide

(Raemark Press: KS, 2018)

This collection of award-winning poems explores a variety of subjects, forms, and styles, including parody. A handy resource for teachers.

"She strings word together in patterns an amateur dreams of." — *The Colony Times*

Arrowhead's Lost Hoard

(The P3 Press: TX, 2008)

Craig must overcome jealousy of his step-siblings, as together they follow the mysterious guest at Lavender Lodge and hunt for buried treasure on a British island.

"Her characters are genuine…" — *Lynne Dibble, school Librarian*

Secret of the Seventh Gate

(Royal Fireworks: NY, 2001)

This story takes readers back forty years to expat life in the Shah's Iran. Fearing loss of friendships—even their lives—kids investigate strange happenings at the mosque and bazaar.

"This book was so exciting I even got up early just to read it." — Joanne (age 8)

www.ingramcontent.com/pod-product-compliance
Lightning Source LLC
LaVergne TN
LVHW072120070426
835511LV00002B/33